D0240640

For 6
4 USD
;B
COPIES

weeded

DK READERS

Pre-level 1

Fishy Tales
Colorful Days
Garden Friends
Party Fun
In the Park
Farm Animals

Petting Zoo
Let's Make Music
Meet the Dinosaurs
Duck Pond Dip
Cuentos de Peces *en español*
Dias Ilenos de color *en español*

Level 1

A Day at Greenhill Farm
Truck Trouble
Tale of a Tadpole
Surprise Puppy!
Duckling Days
A Day at Seagull Beach
Whatever the Weather
Busy Buzzy Bee
Big Machines
Wild Baby Animals
A Bed for the Winter
Born to be a Butterfly
Dinosaur's Day
Feeding Time
Diving Dolphin
Rockets and Spaceships
My Cat's Secret
First Day at Gymnastics

A Trip to the Zoo
I Can Swim!
A Trip to the Library
A Trip to the Doctor
A Trip to the Dentist
I Want To Be A Ballerina
LEGO: Trouble at the Bridge
LEGO: Secret at Dolphin Bay
Star Wars: What is a Wookiee?
A Day in the Life of a Builder
A Day in the Life of a Dancer
A Day in the Life of a Firefighter
A Day in the Life of a Teacher
A Day in the Life of a Musician
A Day in the Life of a Doctor
A Day in the Life of a Police Officer
A Day in the Life of a TV Reporter
Gigantes de Hierro *en español*
Crías del mundo animal *en español*

Level 2

Dinosaur Dinners
Fire Fighter!
Bugs! Bugs! Bugs!
Slinky, Scaly Snakes!
Animal Hospital
The Little Ballerina
Munching, Crunching, Sniffing,
   and Snooping
The Secret Life of Trees
Winking, Blinking, Wiggling,
   and Waggling
Astronaut: Living in Space
Twisters!
Holiday! Celebration Days
   around the World
The Story of Pocahontas
Horse Show
Survivors: The Night the
   Titanic Sank

Eruption! The Story of Volcanoes
The Story of Columbus
Journey of a Humpback Whale
Amazing Buildings
Feathers, Flippers, and Feet
Outback Adventure: Australian
   Vacation
Sniffles, Sneezes, Hiccups, and
   Coughs
Ice Skating Stars
Let's Go Riding
LEGO: Castle Under Attack
LEGO: Rocket Rescue
Star Wars: Journey Through Space
MLB: A Batboy's Day
MLB: Let's Go to the Ballpark!
Spider-Man: Worst Enemies
Meet the X-Men
¡Insectos! *en español*
¡Bomberos! *en español*

A Note to Parents

DK READERS is a compelling program for beginning readers, designed in conjunction with leading literacy experts, including Dr. Linda Gambrell, Professor of Education at Clemson University. Dr. Gambrell has served as President of the National Reading Conference and the College Reading Association, and has recently been elected to serve as President of the International Reading Association.

Beautiful illustrations and superb full-color photographs combine with engaging, easy-to-read stories to offer a fresh approach to each subject in the series.Each DK READER is guaranteed to capture a child's interest while developing his or her reading skills, general knowledge, and love of reading.

The five levels of DK READERS are aimed at different reading abilities, enabling you to choose the books that are exactly right for your child:

Pre-level 1: Learning to read
Level 1: Beginning to read
Level 2: Beginning to read alone
Level 3: Reading alone
Level 4: Proficient readers

The "normal" age at which a child begins to read can be anywhere from three to eight years old. Adult participation through the lower levels is very helpful for providing encouragement, discussing storylines, and sounding out unfamiliar words.

No matter which level you select, you can be sure that you are helping your child learn to read, then read to learn!

LONDON, NEW YORK, MUNICH,
MELBOURNE, AND DELHI

Produced by Southern Lights
Custom Publishing

For DK
Publisher Andrew Berkhut
Executive Editor Andrea Curley
Art Director Tina Vaughan
Photographer Keith Harrelson

Reading Consultant
Linda Gambrell, Ph.D.

First American Edition, 2001
06 10 9 8 7 6
Published in the United States by DK Publishing
375 Hudson Street, New York, New York 10014

Copyright © 2001 Dorling Kindersley Limited

Published in Great Britain by Dorling Kindersley Limited

Library of Congress Cataloging-in-Publication Data

Hayward, Linda.
   A day in the life of a teacher / by Linda Hayward.–
1st American ed.
   p. cm. — (Dorling Kindersley readers)
   Audience: "Level, preschool-grade 1."

ISBN-13: 978-0-7894-7368-4 (hb) ISBN-13: 978-0-7894-7367-7 (pb)

   1. Elementary school teachers—Juvenile literature. 2. Elementary
school teaching--Juvenile literature. [1.Teachers 2. Schools
3. Occupations.] I. Title. II. Series.

LB1776 H39 2001
372.11--dc21

                                        00-055522

Printed and bound in China by L. Rex Printing Co., Ltd.

The characters and events in this story are fictional and
do not represent real persons or events. The author would like
to thank Janis Liss for her help.

All other images © Dorling Kindersley
For more information see: www.dkimages.com

Discover more at
www.dk.com

READERS

BEGINNING
1
TO READ

A Day in the Life of a Teacher

Written by Linda Hayward

DK

DK Publishing

7:00 a.m.

It is time to go to school.
The Hill family gets ready.
Eric and Jason finish breakfast.
Jan Hill fills her tote bag.

Two books,
one lunch,
28 toy fish!

tote bag

Jan teaches second grade.

Jan drives to school.

In the office she
checks her mailbox.
She picks up her
attendance folder.

folder

Time to fix
the calendar!
Today is
Wednesday.

calendar

Before school,
Josh shows
Ms. Hill
his turtle.

Josh was
in her class
last year.

8:00 a.m.
The bell rings.
"Line up here!" says Ms. Hill.
Room Nine lines up.

As they come in, the students put their homework in the basket.

basket

Ms. Hill takes attendance. Ryan is absent.

Hana's reading
group practices
listening skills.

11

The class is learning
about fish.
Ms. Hill passes out
the toy fish.
Then she writes a
word on the board.

dictionary

Who can find
it in the
dictionary?

Brnng!
The fire alarm!
The class lines up
to go outside.

Walking in line
can be hard.

"No pushing!"
says Ms. Hill.

Is it safe to go
back in? Yes!
It was just
a fire drill.

Back in the room, Todd
studies spelling words.

Emily reads
from her journal.

journal

Ms. Hill asks the aide, Ms. Lee, to cut paper for art. "We need 28 of each!" she says. Ms. Hill is planning a bulletin board.

12:00 p.m.

The teachers have lunch together.
They plan their school show.

"The third grade can sing the song about the forest," says Ms. Lopez.

12:30 p.m.

Lunch is over.
A hush falls in Room Nine.
Ms. Hill is reading
a new book of poems.

Now it is time for math.
Ms. Hill has a box.
She takes out one big red square,
one big yellow circle,
and one small yellow circle.

What other shapes are inside?

square

 1:45 p.m.

Jim and Katy learn about graphs.

graph

Jose is working on the computer

Rob has his octopus ready for
the bulletin board.

The school day is almost over.
The students pack up their
homework.

3:00 p.m.

When the bell rings, everyone walks out to the buses.

Ryan's sister comes to pick up his homework. Here is a card that Ryan made for Ms. Hill.

4:30 p.m.

Jan Hill has her own
homework. Her son Eric
helps with the laundry.

Jason serves dinner. It was his turn to cook.

10:00 p.m.

Before she goes to bed,
Jan looks at
Ryan's card again.

She smiles.
She has the best job in the world!

Picture Word List

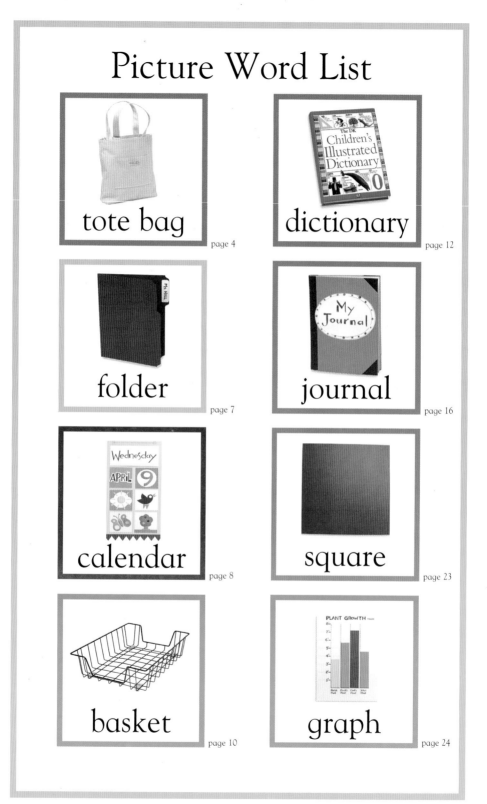

tote bag
page 4

dictionary
page 12

folder
page 7

journal
page 16

calendar
page 8

square
page 23

basket
page 10

graph
page 24